Where Do Babies Come From?

Marcy Schaaf

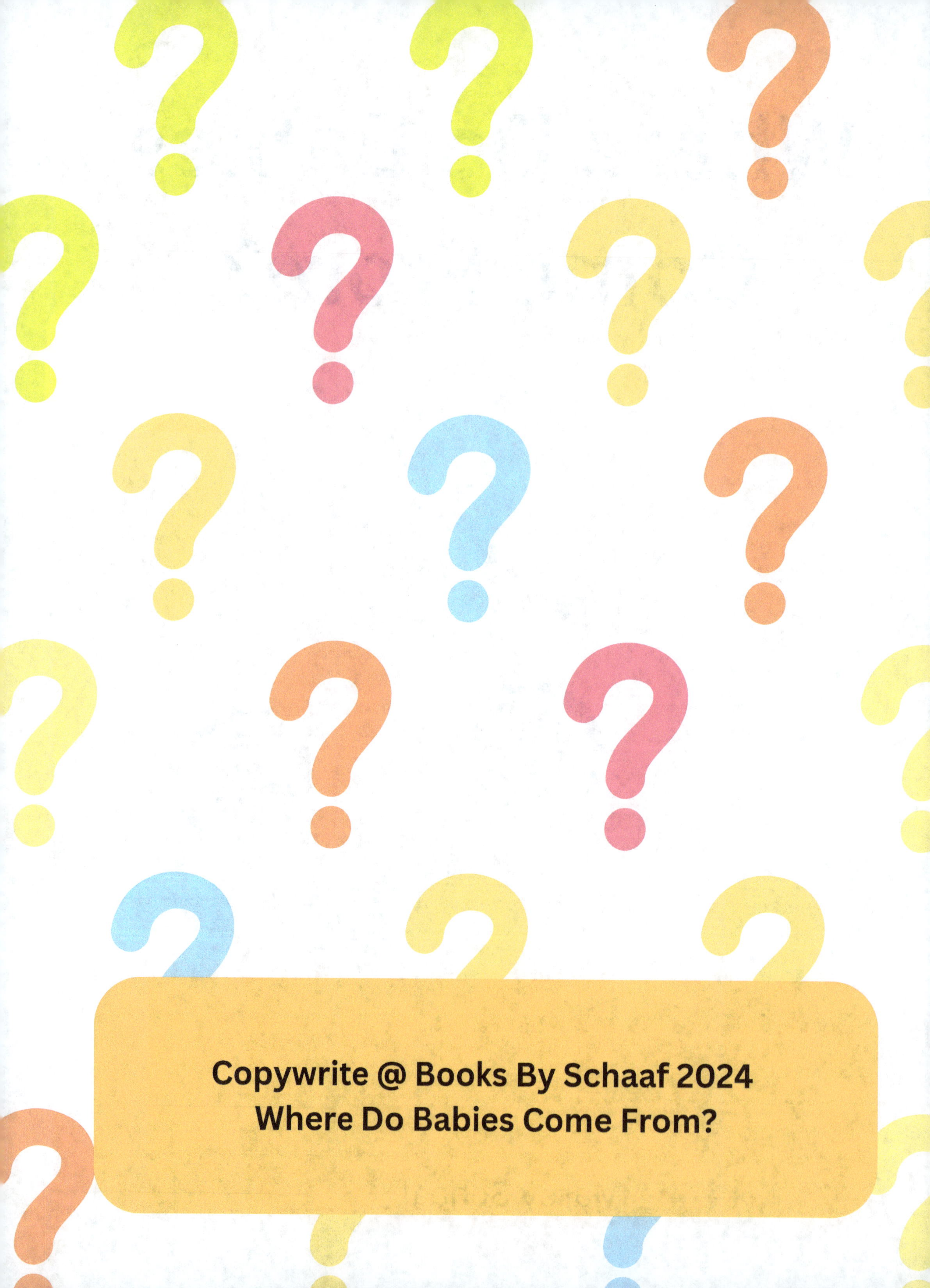

Copywrite @ Books By Schaaf 2024
Where Do Babies Come From?

In the sky so high above.
God sends babies full of love.

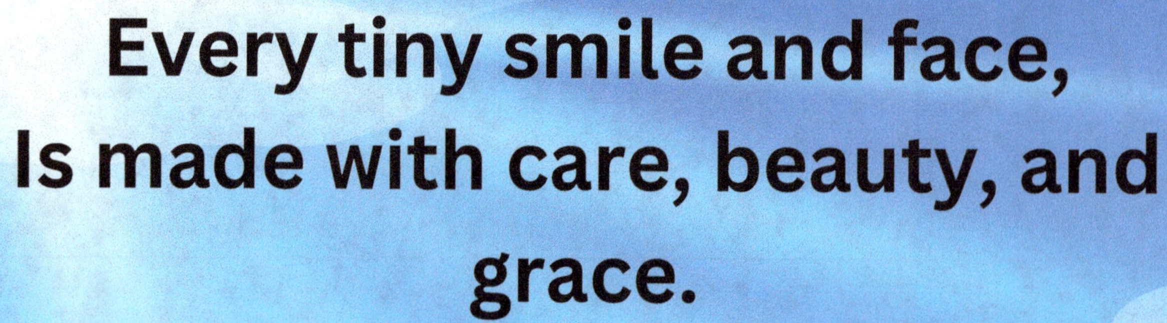
Every tiny smile and face,
Is made with care, beauty, and
grace.

God whispers in the clouds so
bright.
"Here's a gift for hearts so light."

From the stars, He shapes their toes.
Their tiny hands and little nose.

He fills their hearts with joy and cheer.
And makes sure love is always near.

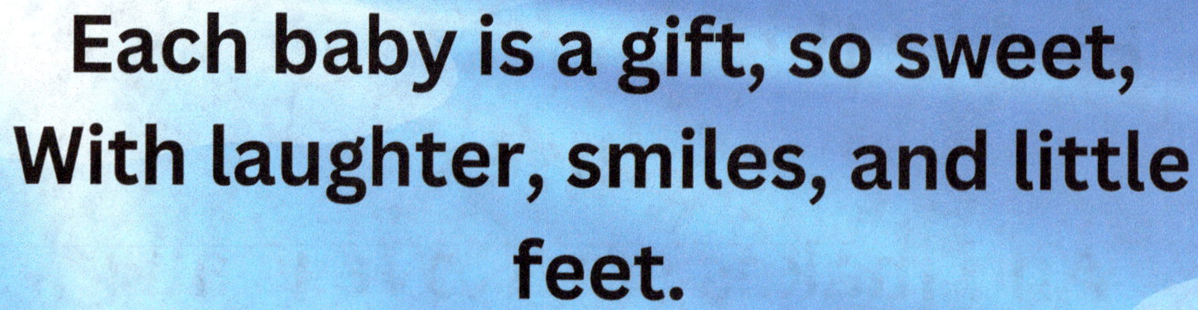

Each baby is a gift, so sweet,
With laughter, smiles, and little feet.

God sends them down for all to
see.
Wrapped in warmth and family.

In every baby, new and small.
There's a piece of God for all.

He sends them down with love so bright.
To fill our days and warm our nights.

Babies come from God's own heart.
A special gift, a perfect start.

From heaven's hands, He lets
them go.
To families waiting here below.

In Mommy's arms, they softly lay.
God's love shining every day.

With Daddy's hugs and gentle care.
God's gift grows strong everywhere.

Brothers, sisters, family, too,
All welcome babies, bright and
new.

God's love fills the house with light.
Making everything feel just right.

So when you ask,
"Where did you come from?"
Just know, you're God's special
one.

God sent you here, full of grace.
To find your home, your perfect
place.

In every laugh, in every tear.
God's love is always near.

So cuddle close and hug real
tight.
God's gifts are pure and full of
light.

You came from love, from God above.
Sent to fill our hearts with love.

Each baby's special, one of a kind.
A gift from God for hearts to find.

He made you perfect, made you true.
And sent you down for me and you.

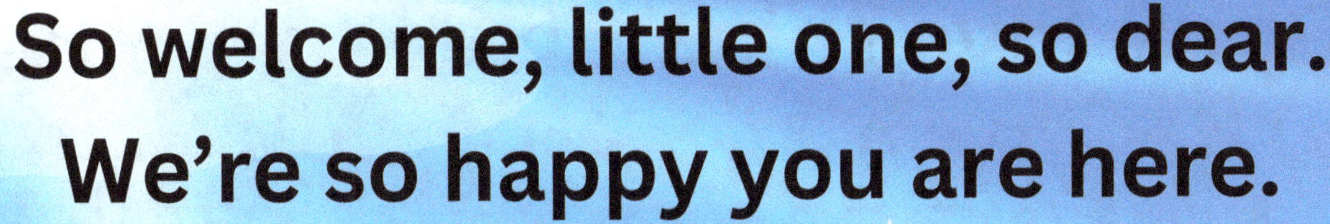

So welcome, little one, so dear.
We're so happy you are here.

God's love shines in every child.
In every grin, soft and mild.

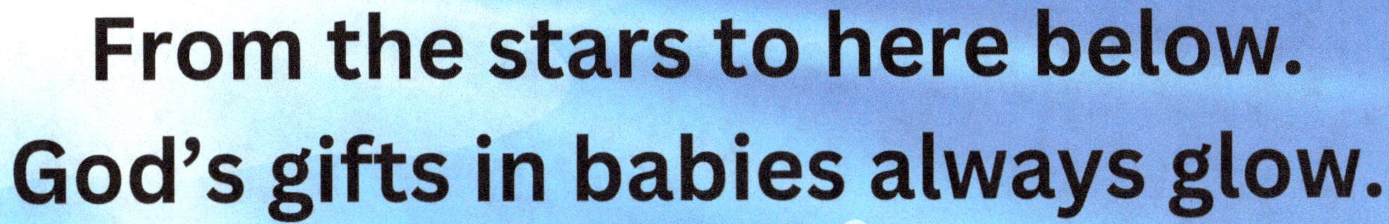

From the stars to here below.
God's gifts in babies always glow.

So when you see a baby small.
Know God sent them to love us
all.

In their laughter, in their eyes.
God's love dances like the skies.

Babies come from God, it's true.
A little gift, just for you.

So let's give thanks, both near
and far.
For God's bright gifts, like shining
stars.

Remember always, every day.
God's love sent you here to stay.

Hold them close, feel their light.
God's gift of love shining bright.

Thank you, God, for babies so
sweet.
Your perfect gift makes life
complete.

Join Our Book of the Month Club!

Looking for the perfect gift that keeps on giving? Join our Book of the Month Club! For just $25 a month, or $250 if you purchase a year upfront, you or your loved ones will receive a handpicked children's book every month, straight to your doorstep.

Here's how it works:
Choose from 15 different languages to receive bilingual books that make learning fun.
Enjoy monthly shipments of our exclusive books that inspire, teach, and entertain children of all ages.
Each month's book is carefully selected to provide a new adventure, valuable lesson, and a chance to explore cultures from around the world.
It's the perfect gift for birthdays, holidays, or just because! Whether you're nurturing a young reader or encouraging language learning, our Book of the Month Club is designed to bring joy to every bookshelf.

Exclusive Bonus: As part of your membership, you'll also receive a monthly podcast about our featured book delivered straight to your email! Listen in for behind-the-scenes insights, fun facts, and tips for making storytime even more magical.

Sign up today at www.Booksbyschaaf.com and start enjoying the gift of reading all year long!

Books By Schaaf

www.BookBySchaaf.com

Find us at:

www.ingramcontent.com/pod-product-compliance
Lightning Source LLC
Chambersburg PA
CBHW08081120726

48001CB00009B/2940